THE HANDY LITTLE GUIDE

Liturgy of the Hours

Barb Sz

OSV

Our Sunday Visitor
Huntington, Indiana

Nihil Obstat
Msgr. Michael Heintz, Ph.D.
Censor Librorum

Imprimatur
✠ Kevin C. Rhoades
Bishop of Fort Wayne-South Bend
November 16, 2022

The *Nihil Obstat* and *Imprimatur* are official declarations that a book is free from doctrinal or moral error. It is not implied that those who have granted the *Nihil Obstat* and *Imprimatur* agree with the contents, opinions, or statements expressed.

28 27 26 25 24 23 1 2 3 4 5 6 7 8 9

Our Sunday Visitor Publishing Division
Our Sunday Visitor, Inc.
200 Noll Plaza
Huntington, IN 46750 www.osv.com
1-800-348-2440

ISBN: 978-1-63966-029-2 (Inventory No. T2771)
1. RELIGION—Christian Living—Prayer.
2. RELIGION—Christian Living—Spiritual Growth.
3. RELIGION—Christianity—Catholic.

eISBN: 978-1-63966-031-5
LCCN: 2022950534

Cover design and Interior design: Amanda Falk
Cover art and Interior art: AdobeStock

PRINTED IN THE UNITED STATES OF AMERICA

Contents

1
What Is the Liturgy of the Hours?

The Liturgy of the Hours is a form of common prayer that, like the Mass, is standard (universal) throughout the Roman Catholic Church. *Common prayer* means that it is often prayed within groups, though many people can and do pray the Liturgy of the Hours on their own. Whether it is prayed alone or in common, the Liturgy of the Hours unites those in prayer with the whole Church. In that way, no one prays the Liturgy of the Hours alone, because throughout the world everyone is praying the same prayers.

The Liturgy of the Hours follows a daily rhythm of prayer through the liturgical year. Based on a cyclical recitation of the psalms, it is also rich in Scripture from other books of the Old and New Testaments. The Liturgy of the Hours originally developed from the Jewish practice of praying three times daily, which was integrated into the prayer life of the early Church. The custom of praying at fixed times per day was modified and refined during the monastic age, when St. Benedict organized what was then called the Divine Office into a system of prayer every three hours around the clock. This required enormous books that had to be hand-copied and that were kept in monastery chapels. Smaller, portable books known as *breviaries* came into fashion in the Middle Ages for newly founded religious orders which traveled to preach and teach.

In the 1960s, the Second Vatican Council issued the latest major revision to the Divine Office, simplifying it and calling for it to be prayed in every language, so that all of the faithful could participate in the prayer of the Church without needing to know Latin. "When the faithful are invited to the Liturgy of the Hours and come together in unity of heart and voice, they show forth the Church in its celebration of the mystery of Christ."* While the sacrifice of the Eucharist can only be offered by a priest, the Liturgy of the Hours is a sacrifice of praise that can be offered by anyone.

To pray the Liturgy of the Hours, you'll need a *breviary*. This book (or set of books, depending on the format you choose) contains the psalms and prayers used in the Liturgy of the Hours and instructions for praying them according to the norms for each day of the liturgical year. There is a learning curve, but you get to pray as you learn — and learn as you pray. Even if you don't get all the details right every time while you're learning, you are still praying.

---

* Congregation for Divine Worship, *General Instruction of the Liturgy of the Hours* (Washington, DC: United States Conference of Catholic Bishops, 2002), 22.

Yes, praying the Liturgy of the Hours can be complicated, but don't worry: We're going to walk together through the basics of this beautiful way to pray.

2 Discovering the Liturgy of the Hours

I first discovered Liturgy of the Hours as a college student. On retreats, the campus ministry director led us through Morning and Evening Prayer. And on Sunday evenings, the chaplain began a tradition of Benediction and Night Prayer. Some friends and I, wanting to pray the Hours more regularly, saved our spending money to purchase the single-volume *Christian Prayer* edition of the breviary and met to pray Morning Prayer a few days a week.

I continued praying Morning and Evening Prayer on my own through graduate school and into the early years of my marriage and motherhood — sometimes sporadically, depending on my life circumstances. When I began formation as a Secular Franciscan, I learned that these two Hours were part of the prayer discipline of the order. I already had the single-volume breviary and knew the basics of using it, so it was easy to recommit to the twice-daily prayer routine. That was more than twenty years ago.

After college, I usually prayed the Hours on my own, unless I was attending a Secular Franciscan gathering where we prayed in common. Then, when the world shut down at the beginning of the coronavirus pandemic in March 2020, my husband purchased a four-volume breviary and asked me to teach him to pray Evening Prayer. Since that time, we have prayed together each day, usually after we've finished dinner and cleaned up the kitchen. We pray Morning Prayer on our own.

When I first discovered that for the Liturgy of the Hours, as with almost any other activity, there were apps for that, I eagerly said, "Take my money!" to the creators of two such apps and tucked away my *Christian Prayer* on the living room bookcase. The lure of the shiny, convenient app that took all the guesswork out of praying the Liturgy of the Hours was strong, and I was a busy mom in a season of life when convenience took precedence over the flexibility the book version offered. It was years before I bothered to pick up my bound breviary again.

I finally made the switch back to using the books after feeling disappointed (repeatedly) that the apps didn't offer the prayers for the celebration of some saints to whom I have a devotion. For me, the convenience of an app is nice when I'm traveling, but I don't prefer to pray this way on a daily basis. The feel of holding the book, turning the pages, setting up the ribbons, and finding a random holy card here and there — along with the flexibility to exercise the option of celebrating favorite saints listed as "optional" — made this an easy decision for me.

Several years ago, I rescued a damaged four-volume breviary that had been donated to my parish library. The library volunteers had set the books aside to be destroyed because the bindings of all four volumes had completely separated from the covers. Judging by the different cover styles, the books had come from at least two separate sets, but all four volumes were there. With permission, I took them home and glued them back together, leaving the newly glued volumes unopened for several weeks to ensure the best chance that the repair would hold.

Since that time, I've begun using those books for daily prayer. I re-glued the Advent/ Christmas book last winter and replaced the ribbons in all four volumes, and I keep the book I'm using right now in a cloth cover for extra protection.

My edition of *Christian Prayer* is newer than these books, and I could, if I wanted, purchase a new four-volume set. Yet these are the books I find myself drawn to use. My *Christian Prayer* book has no torn edges or folded corners on the pages, and in comparison to these old books, is clean and pretty.

Something about these well-prayed pages, though, appeals to me more than that newer, cleaner book.

These breviary pages have a history I'll never know. Sometimes I remember to pray for their previous owner, the one whose hands and prayers softened the pages containing the familiar psalms. Sometimes I remember that just as I'm connected to the present-day Church, praying the Liturgy of the Hours at the same time but in different places, I'm also connected to all who have prayed before me — including the one who first owned my breviary — and all who will pray with it in the future.

3
Why Pray This Way?

Anyone can pray the Liturgy of the Hours. The Vatican II document *Sacrosanctum Concilium* encourages priests to provide opportunities to pray some of the Hours in common in the parish, and invites lay people to participate as a group or on their own: "Pastors of souls should see to it that the chief hours, especially Vespers, are celebrated in common in church on Sundays and the more solemn feasts. And the laity, too, are encouraged to recite the divine office, either with the priests, or among themselves, or even individually."*

* *Sacrosanctum Concilium*, vatican.va, par. 100; also in Austin Flannery, OP, ed., *Vatican Council II: The Conciliar and Post Conciliar Documents* (Collegeville, MN: The Liturgical Press, 1975).

While it takes a bit of time to learn to pray the Liturgy of the Hours, help is available in a variety of ways (including this little book!). Beginners can benefit from parishes or groups that pray in common and help members learn to use the breviary, as well as periodicals, smartphone apps, and radio broadcasts that allow one to pray along without worrying about the details of handling ribbons and flipping pages. Later, we'll explore some of these options and how these tools can simplify the learning process.

Priests, deacons, and men and women religious are required to pray the five main Hours each day. Some lay people, such as members of third orders and other institutes for the laity, pray certain Hours as a rule. But you don't have to be ordained, take religious vows, or become a member of a lay institute to pray the Liturgy of the Hours: Everyone is invited. After concluding a series on the psalms in his general audiences, Pope Benedict XVI encouraged the faithful: "I would … like to renew to you all the invitation to pray with the Psalms, even becoming accustomed to using the Liturgy of the Hours of the Church, Lauds in the morning, Vespers in the evening, and Compline before retiring."*

Just as the Eucharistic liturgy — the Mass — has some elements that remain the same but others that vary from day to day and season to season, the Liturgy of the Hours is not the same every day, or every Sunday, or even every first Sunday of the month. In the same way that you learned how to respond at Mass and when to sit, stand, and kneel by attending Mass and following the example of others, you will learn to pray the Liturgy of the Hours by praying.

But Why Should I?

Praying the Liturgy of the Hours regularly will keep you attuned to the liturgical year. You'll observe how the prayers, readings,

*Benedict XVI, General Audience, November 16, 2011, vatican.va.

and other elements of the various hours change throughout the seasons — and while the psalms themselves remain the same, you'll focus on different aspects of them at different times in the Church year. The liturgical year brings variety, while the repetition of the psalms provides familiarity in a beautiful balance.

At the same time, you'll begin to notice connections to the Mass, with certain prayers and Scripture verses appearing during Mass and in the Liturgy of the Hours on the same day of the liturgical year. This is all part of the continuity of prayer inherent in the Catholic liturgy.

By praying the Liturgy of the Hours, you'll be following St. Paul's advice to "pray without ceasing" (1 Thes 5:17). You can sanctify various times of day, and you'll be doing so with the whole Church, whether you're alone or in a small group.

The Liturgy of the Hours is a point of connection through prayer with others all over the world praying the same prayers and the same psalms. One day, a friend of mine who was beginning to learn to pray the Liturgy of the Hours took her husband to a hospital for a surgical procedure. Early that morning I texted her to let her know I was praying for him. She replied to thank me, and to verify that she was beginning Morning Prayer in the right place. Once we sorted out those details, I let her know that, as I was also ready to begin Morning Prayer, we would be praying simultaneously. We weren't physically together, but we were still praying together.

As you pray the Liturgy of the Hours, you'll become more familiar with Scripture — and plenty of it. Almost all of the 150 psalms are included in the breviary, as well as three Gospel canticles and brief selections from other parts of Scripture. God speaks to us, even today, through Scripture. When we pray using Scripture, we will find new meaning even in familiar verses. As our circumstances change, God emphasizes his message in a new way every day and in every season.

You'll also become more familiar with the saints as you pray the Liturgy of the Hours, because the liturgical year includes celebration of saints as well as the seasons of Advent, Christmas, Ordinary Time, Lent, and Easter. On some feast days, you'll have the opportunity to read from primary sources by or about a particular saint, and on every feast day, there's a short biography of the saint(s) for that day.

4
Overcoming the Obstacles

It's no secret that praying the Liturgy of the Hours involves a learning process. Certainly, there are easier ways to pray. You'll also need equipment: access to a breviary and, when you're getting started, assistance from helpful individuals or published prayer aids to keep you on the right page (literally). Once you have the equipment, though, the challenge is not insurmountable. There are many resources available — often free or at low cost — to help you along the way.

Learning to pray the Liturgy of the Hours, even if you choose to pray only one of the Hours of the day, is well worth the challenge. Many people repeat variations on the theme "It's *so* hard!" when they tell me why they gave up praying the Liturgy of the Hours after only a few attempts. They're right; it doesn't come easy at first. Neither does driving a car, baking bread from scratch, or learning to write your name. Like those skills and many others, this form of prayer requires patience, perseverance, and practice.

I've seen the Liturgy of the Hours described as "impractical." On the contrary: The Liturgy of the Hours is beautifully practical, as it's integrated into the liturgical calendar. It is no more impractical than the Mass. Both the Mass and the Liturgy of the Hours, as prayers of the Church, follow similar patterns of prayer based on a well-defined calendar of seasons and celebrations of saints. As a pragmatic person who appreciates systems and logic, I appreciate and admire the structure of the Liturgy of the Hours.

Is it worth the effort? Yes. Is it doable? *Yes!* Start small, both in building the habit of prayer and your skills in navigating the breviary. Night Prayer is a wonderful way to begin, because it's shorter and less complex than Morning and Evening Prayer. Take all the time you need to build up your prayer muscles. Enlist the help of a friend as you get started — or for the times when you lose your place in the liturgical calendar. Gradually, you'll be able to pray your way through the liturgical day, week, and year with less assistance from friends or published guides.

This Book Looks Really Complicated

Before you begin to pray the Liturgy of the Hours, you'll need a bit of a guided tour through the breviary — we'll talk more about different breviary formats in the next chapter — and an explanation of some commonly used terms. We're looking at *Christian Prayer: The Liturgy of the Hours* (the one-volume version). The format in *Christian Prayer* is easier for a beginner to use, and the single book is much less expensive to purchase than the four-volume edition of the Liturgy of the Hours, which has a slightly different setup and includes the full versions of Office of Readings and Daytime Prayer. We'll discuss that format, as well as other options for praying the Liturgy of the Hours, later.

Christian Prayer begins with an abridged version of the *General Instruction of the Liturgy of the Hours*. This explains the prayer's importance in the life of the Church, how praying the Liturgy of the Hours is a way to pray without ceasing, and an exhortation that everyone in the Church can (and should be encouraged to) pray in this way.

Next is a table listing the "movable feasts" of the liturgical year, so called because their dates change year to year. This chart details the dates for Ash Wednesday, Easter, Ascension, Pentecost, Corpus Christi, and the First Sunday of Advent, as well as the end of Ordinary Time before Lent and the beginning of Ordinary Time after Easter.

The *General Roman Calendar* is a month-by-month listing of feast days: solemnities, feasts, memorials, and optional memorials. It's worth keeping a little holy card as a bookmark on the page for the current month, so you can easily flip to this section to see what each day will bring.

The *General Principles* provide some of the rules of thumb, called *rubrics*, for the celebration of the hours. This explains the basics of how to pray each hour. More complete rubrics can be found in the *General Instruction of the Liturgy of the Hours*, and the rubrics in the breviary include paragraph numbers if you wish to make a deeper dive into the how-tos.

Next is the *Proper of Seasons*. This part of the breviary contains prayers, readings, psalms, and antiphons (more on those in a bit) that are specific to particular seasons of the liturgical year: Advent, Christmas, Ordinary Time, Lent (including the Triduum), and Easter. This seasonal content frequently echoes prayers and readings of the Mass. All year 'round, the Proper of Seasons contains antiphons for the Gospel canticles and closing prayer for Sundays. That's all you'll find in the Proper of Seasons during Ordinary Time, but throughout the seasons of Advent, Christmas, Lent, and Easter, the Proper of Seasons is packed with weekday content as well: antiphons for the psalms and canticles, plus everything from the reading through the end of the Hour.

The *Ordinary* follows. *Ordinary* here refers to the order in which things are done, not Ordinary Time. For the Liturgy of the Hours beginner, the Ordinary is an important place in the book, and I recommend keeping a holy card or other bookmark for this section. You'll refer to it often, as it contains a psalm and some seasonal antiphons for the Invitatory (the first Hour of the day); a walk-through of each Hour including when to flip to the Proper of Seasons, Proper of Saints, or Common of Saints; and the Gospel canticles for Morning and Evening Prayer. The Ordinary is filled with instructions to help you through each of the Hours. As you become more familiar with the format, you'll need to consult this section less and less.

The *Psalter* is the section of the breviary containing the four-week cycle of psalms, readings, and prayers for Morning and Evening Prayer. It has been arranged so that Week I of the cycle coincides with the first weeks of Advent, Ordinary Time, and Lent, and Week II coincides with the Second Week of Easter. Roman numerals are used to designate the numbers of the weeks within the psalter.

The *Daytime Prayer* section of the breviary includes prayers and psalms for midmorning, midday, and midafternoon.

Night Prayer for each day of the week follows, with the antiphons in honor of the Blessed Virgin Mary at the end of that section.

The *Proper of Saints* goes month by month through the calendar year, with information about the saints celebrated each day and special antiphons, readings, and prayers. You'll see that certain saints have more proper content than others: For example, St. Sebastian (January 20) has a proper prayer, but St. Agnes (January 21) has proper content for nearly everything in Morning and Evening Prayer. The Proper of Saints also directs you to the corresponding section in the Common of Saints for some prayer content.

The *Commons* (Common of Saints) contain prayer content that certain categories of saints have in common. Saints are celebrated as apostles, martyrs (singly or as a group), pastors (priests, bishops, and popes), Doctors of the Church, virgins, holy men, or holy women. There are also subsections for religious, those who worked for the underprivileged, and teachers. Within the Common of Saints are also prayers for the celebration of the dedication of a church and celebrations of the Blessed Virgin Mary.

The *Office for the Dead* is the only section of the Liturgy of the Hours that is not dedicated to a particular time in the liturgical or calendar year. All Hours of the Office for the Dead are in the same section.

Hymns for the celebration of all the Hours follow. Each Hour has suggested hymns, and there is a table with hymn selections for the Proper of Seasons, Proper and Commons of the Saints, and Office for the Dead. This section also offers music, or psalm tones, for the psalms, prayers, and blessings in the Liturgy of the Hours, for communities who chant the Hours. If you're praying alone, you can choose to listen to the hymn from an online source rather than singing it.

An abbreviated version of the *Office of Readings* follows. Only the four-volume Liturgy of the Hours contains the full Office of Readings.

Christian Prayer concludes with an appendix of devotional poetry, a chart of the two-year cycle of Scripture passages for the Office of Readings, and an index of psalms, index of canticles, index of biblical readings, index of non-biblical readings, a listing of hymns, and an alphabetical index of celebrations.

Another essential resource is the small booklet titled *St. Joseph Guide for the Liturgy of the Hours*, produced by Catholic Book Publishing. The *St. Joseph Guide* lists all the celebrations for each day and provides the page numbers where you'll need to set your ribbons before beginning to pray. It's known as a "cheat sheet" in some circles, but there's no cheating involved and no shame in using this kind of resource. This guide will keep you in the right place at the right time. It runs through the entire calendar year and is published in different editions for the four-volume Liturgy of the Hours and *Christian Prayer;* if you use this guide, you will need to purchase a new one every year, available online at catholicbookpublishing.com and at your local Catholic bookseller.

What Do These Words Even Mean?

An *antiphon* is recited at the beginning and end of a psalm or canticle, like the refrain of a song.

Canticles are Scripture selections that

are used in the same way as psalms; you'll see that they're printed in verse format instead of prose format, even though some canticles are expressed as prose in the Bible.

A *psalmody* is a collection of particular psalms to be prayed at a certain time — that is, the psalmody for Morning Prayer is different from the one for Evening Prayer.

Each psalm or canticle is divided into *strophes*: small groups of verses ranging from two to six lines. When groups pray the Liturgy of the Hours, the group divides in two, with each half taking turns reciting strophes and the Glory to the Father prayer at the end of each psalm or canticle.

A *responsory* follows the reading in each Hour, though it is generally longer in Morning and Evening Prayer and the Office of Readings. Often the responsory includes repeating a line or part of a line — if you are praying by yourself, you can skip that repetition.

5
Formats for Praying

There are four different editions of the Liturgy of the Hours. The largest and most complete format is the four-volume set, with separate books for Advent/Christmas, Lent/Easter, Ordinary Time weeks one through seventeen, and Ordinary Time weeks eighteen through thirty-four. The four-volume set contains the full texts for all the Hours and is most often used by priests and those in religious communities.

Christian Prayer is a single large book with the complete texts for Morning and Evening Prayer for all liturgical seasons and feast days, the Office for the Dead, and Night Prayer. It also contains selections from Daytime Prayer and the Office of Readings. As the selections are more limited in scope, if you pray those Hours from *Christian Prayer*, you may not always match up with the priests and religious and any laity who are using the four-volume edition.

Shorter Christian Prayer contains the complete texts for Morning and Evening Prayer for all liturgical seasons, plus Night Prayer and Office for the Dead. This edition includes very few feast days: only selected feasts of the Blessed Virgin Mary, plus the feasts of St. Joseph, St. John the Baptist, the Triumph of the Cross, All Saints' Day, and the Dedication of St. John Lateran are found in this book.

The four-volume *Liturgy of the Hours*, *Christian Prayer*, and *Shorter Christian Prayer* are all available in large-print editions, and the page numbers of those editions match the standard-size books.

Daytime Prayer includes midmorning, midday, and midafternoon prayer. This small prayer book is easy to keep in your briefcase, tote, or desk at work.

Night Prayer, as the title suggests, contains only Night Prayer. It's an excellent, inexpensive option for families who pray this Hour together or for anyone who wants to keep it at their bedside for end-of-day prayers.

Breviary supplements are available, and these include newly canonized saints and other newly established feast days. These supplements contain only the proper prayers and readings for those feasts; they do not stand on their own as prayer books.

Beyond breviaries, you'll find periodicals, apps, and audio versions of the Hours, both as podcasts or radio programs. If you're able to find audio that contains the full Hour, this is a good way to become familiar with the format of the prayers. It may even whet your appetite to begin praying the Liturgy of the Hours regularly.

Non-breviary alternatives for praying Liturgy of the Hours often describe themselves as less expensive and easier to use than the breviary itself. There is a price for convenience, however, and that price includes the flexibility to choose to celebrate an optional memorial, or which feast to celebrate if two or more are on the calendar for the same date. When you are using *Christian Prayer* or the four-volume *Liturgy of the Hours*, all those options are available to you.

Some periodicals provide a modified (often shortened) version of Morning and Evening Prayer. This is fine for personal devotion, but be sure to note that if you are praying with others, these versions won't match up to the breviary. Other non-breviary versions of Liturgy of the Hours use different translations of psalms and readings, which becomes an obstacle when praying in a group. For group prayer, always be sure before you start that everyone is using the same edition! As with periodicals, do your research before investing in an app or a paid subscription to a podcast; ensure that it provides the format you want.

You might think that a periodical containing the prayers of the Liturgy of the

Hours is less expensive than a breviary, but that is only true for a short while. Eventually, you'll have spent the same money but have nothing to show for it but a pile of outdated magazines you might be reluctant to recycle, but which you won't be able to use in future years. A breviary is more expensive up front, but the more you pray it, the more value you get for that money: That book (or set of books) will last you a lifetime.

Finally, while accessing the Liturgy of the Hours in an app on your smartphone or tablet or on a website takes the guesswork out of figuring out what page you're on, it also puts you in front of a screen. That often leads to its own set of distractions: Giving in to the temptation to check email or scroll through social media before praying might eat up your prayer time before you even have the chance to begin. And when you close that app or browser tab, everything else is in front of you once again. Using a breviary, completely dedicated only to prayer, you'll allow yourself the opportunity to make a slower, more natural transition between prayer time and work, play, rest, or family life.

While shortened versions of the Liturgy of the Hours, podcasts, apps, or periodicals have their place, it's my hope that these become entry points for people who want to learn to pray the Hours as they are prayed throughout the Church. They're convenient, easier to learn, and accessible, but they have their limitations. Don't be discouraged if you're unable to get the hang of all the details of using the breviary right away. What matters is that you try — and that you're praying.

6
What Are the Hours?

No, you don't need hours upon hours every day to pray the Divine Office. They are called "Hours" because they occur at regularly appointed times — like the phrase *dinner hour* refers to the time your family eats dinner, which probably doesn't take an hour either. Some Hours are longer than others, with the Office of Readings being the lengthiest one and Night Prayer the shortest at five to ten minutes. Of course, you'll need a bit more time in the beginning as you become familiar with the routine, and praying aloud in a group takes a little longer than reading the prayers silently by yourself.

Invitatory

The day's prayers begin with the *Invitatory*, a call to gather and praise God. The Invitatory is one psalm long, plus its antiphon. You can pray the Invitatory all on its own or as a lead-in to the Office of Readings or Morning Prayer. The breviary contains rules about how to begin those other Hours with the Invitatory.

Four psalms can be used for the Invitatory: Psalm 95, which is the default option; Psalm 100; Psalm 67; and Psalm 24. These last three are sometimes prayed during other hours; if that happens, Psalm 95 should be substituted in that place. While the Invitatory psalms do not change during the liturgical year, the antiphons reflect the feasts and seasons of the Church.

Office of Readings

The Office of Readings, which can be prayed at any time of day, includes:

- a hymn

- three psalms and their antiphons
- two readings with a responsory after each
- the *Te Deum* — sometimes; the rubrics in the book will note when it's included
- a closing prayer

The first of the two readings comes from the Bible, but the second comes from the rich spiritual writings of the Church: selections from the writings of the Church Fathers and Doctors of the Church as well as saints or writers with associations with particular saints. Through these readings, you'll come to have a greater understanding of salvation history and the various saints of the Church.

Morning Prayer (Lauds)

Morning Prayer includes:

- a hymn
- psalm and antiphon

- Old Testament canticle and antiphon
- second psalm and antiphon
- a reading from Scripture
- responsory
- Gospel canticle and its antiphon
- intercessions
- closing prayer

The Canticle of Zechariah is the Gospel canticle for Morning Prayer.

Daytime Prayer

Daytime Prayer contains three separate Hours; you may choose to pray one, two, or all three. The first Hour you pray will follow the current psalmody, based on the days of the week; if you choose to pray more than one hour in Daytime Prayer, you'll use the complementary psalmody. Daytime Prayer includes:

- hymn
- two psalms and their antiphons

(from either the current or complementary psalmody)
- Scripture reading
- responsory verse
- closing prayer

Evening Prayer (Vespers)

Evening Prayer includes:

- hymn
- two psalms (or one longer psalm divided into two parts) and their antiphons
- New Testament canticle and antiphon
- New Testament reading
- responsory
- Gospel canticle and its antiphon
- intercessions
- closing prayer

The Magnificat is the Gospel canticle for Evening Prayer.

Night Prayer (Compline)

Night Prayer includes:

- brief period of examination of conscience
- one or two psalms and antiphons
- reading from Scripture
- responsory
- Gospel canticle and its antiphon
- closing prayer
- antiphon to the Blessed Virgin Mary (a selection of these is provided in both Latin and English)

The Canticle of Simeon is the Gospel canticle for Night Prayer.

What's the Difference Between Evening Prayer I and II?

In the same way as the celebration of Sunday or a solemnity begins the evening before with a Vigil Mass, the Church begins the prayers appropriate for that celebration the evening before with Evening Prayer I. That's why you won't see prayers labeled "Saturday, Evening Prayer." On Saturday evening, we pray Evening Prayer I for Sunday; we pray Evening Prayer II for Sunday on Sunday evening.

We do the same for solemnities that occur during the week. This means that you will need to pay a bit of attention to the liturgical calendar as you go along, because it's easy to miss Evening Prayer I for a solemnity you didn't realize was coming up.

This practice stems from Jewish Sabbath law: the Sabbath celebration begins on Friday evening, the day before the actual Sabbath Day. The Church celebrates solemnities, which include Sundays, beginning on the evening of the day before.

7
What Time Do I Pray the Hours?

There is not a specific time of day, down to the hour and minute, that particular Hours must be prayed. This varies according to the circumstances of the one praying. Some people might pray Morning Prayer when they first wake up. Others sleep later — or pray later, perhaps arriving at church a little early for daily Mass and praying Morning Prayer at that time. Vowed religious living in communities will have standard times for daily prayer, but lay people don't generally follow a monastic schedule.

The **Invitatory** is the first prayer of the day. Pray it just before you pray Morning Prayer or the Office of Readings (if you pray this Hour), whichever comes first. Or pray it on its own, then return to pray another Hour later.

Office of Readings can be prayed at any time of the day.

Morning Prayer is traditionally prayed at dawn, but you can pray it whenever you begin your day.

Daytime Prayer is prayed in the middle of the day. There are three options: midmorning, midday, and midafternoon. You may choose to pray one or all of these brief hours.

Evening Prayer concludes the work day. *Evening* means different things to different people. Some people pray Evening Prayer right after work. In my home, we usually pray it after we've eaten dinner and cleaned up the kitchen, and before we move on to other after-dinner activities or evening commitments outside the home.

Night Prayer is prayed at bedtime.

Some of the prayers of the Hours truly are related to the time of day in which the

Hour is prayed. The intercessions for Morning Prayer, for example, are geared toward dedicating our day to God and living it in a way that honors and glorifies him. Later, during Evening Prayer, we pray for others — and we always conclude those intercessions by praying for the dead. Because the prayers and other content in certain Hours are time-sensitive, it's best to strive to pray as close to the correct part of the day as you can.

8
The Four-Week Cycle and the Five Seasons

The *Psalter*, or collection of psalms and canticles used in the Liturgy of the Hours, is set up on a four-week cycle for Morning and Evening Prayer and the Office of Readings. Every four weeks, we begin at the beginning and pray the prayers for Week I. This means there's repetition of psalms and other parts of the Hours each month. But even as the various feasts and seasons of the Church bring variety, this repetition brings familiarity. When the psalms, canticles, or other readings from the Bible come up as readings during Mass, you'll recognize them. Over time, you may even come to memorize them.

Despite the repetition, something about

the Liturgy of the Hours feels new every time. As the prayers, psalms, readings, and antiphons are prayed at different times of the year, you'll find that the same line of Scripture hits different, depending on the Church year — and even your own circumstances. For example, during most of the year the antiphon for Psalm 51 on Friday of Week II is "A humble, contrite heart, O God, you will not spurn." This emphasizes the contrition that is central to this psalm. But during the Easter season, the antiphon is "Have courage, my son; your sins are forgiven, alleluia." The Easter antiphon celebrates the forgiveness of sin that is the result of Christ's sacrifice on the cross.

Of all the seasons within the liturgical year, Ordinary Time is easiest when it comes to the Liturgy of the Hours. On a weekday without any feast-day celebrations, you'll pray Morning and Evening Prayer straight through without needing to flip to other parts of the book, except for the Gospel canticles. (Eventually you'll memorize those canticles, as they're prayed every single day, regardless of season.) There are special antiphons for Sunday Evening Prayer I, Morning Prayer, and Evening Prayer II for each Sunday of the year, as well as closing prayers, and all of those are found in the Proper of Seasons.

During the seasons of Advent, Christmas, Lent, and Easter, you will need to refer to the Proper of Seasons during Morning and Evening Prayer each day, for everything after the psalms and canticle.

What Week Is This?

You don't simply begin at Week I the first time you open the breviary. The cycle corresponds to the Church's liturgical year. So how do you make sure you're praying in the right place? The simplest option is to check the *St. Joseph Guide* or online to verify the right place to begin. Remember, it's not cheating to use resources like this: They are intended to help you as you become accustomed to praying the Liturgy of the Hours.

The resources available will also tell you

whether you are in Week I, II, III, or IV of the Psalter. Thankfully, you only have to find this information once — and then you keep cycling through until you reach a new liturgical season.

9
Level Up! Solemnities, Feasts, and Memorials

The liturgical calendar includes a hierarchy of special days. The all-purpose term *feast day* actually comprises four levels: solemnities, feasts, memorials, and optional memorials. These are listed in order of prominence. When more than one occasion is slated for the same day, the Church has provided guidance in a Table of Liturgical Days[*] which states the order of precedence. This allows for some flexibility. For example, if a saint who is the titular saint of the parish is

*The Table of Liturgical Days is printed in the four-volume *Liturgy of the Hours* but not in *Christian Prayer.* It is also available online at http://www.romcal.net/norms.html.

normally celebrated as an optional memorial, it moves up in the rankings to a *proper solemnity* and therefore would be celebrated ahead of another saint's feast day.

If two or three saints' days of similar rank are scheduled for the same date, you (or the group you're praying with) may select the one you wish to celebrate. It's an easy call when you have a devotion to a particular saint. When that's not the case, you can make a random choice, or honor one saint in the morning and the other in the evening, or alternate years.

A **solemnity,** the highest-ranking celebration, begins with Evening Prayer I the day before — and if the solemnity is a holy day of obligation, there's probably a Vigil Mass being celebrated at your parish, with three readings, the Gloria, and the Creed. The rubrics for Morning Prayer for a solemnity will direct you to pray the psalms from Sunday morning, Week I, and you'll follow the instructions within the Proper of Saints and/or the Commons for everything else. If a solemnity occurs on a Sunday in Ordinary Time, that solemnity will take precedence over the Sunday. In Advent or Lent, the solemnity is celebrated on Monday of the same week. In addition, Sundays are always categorized as solemnities — that's why we pray Evening Prayer I for each Sunday.

On a **feast,** as on solemnities, everything is taken from the Proper of Saints and/or the Commons. You will not be using anything from the current weekday in the psalter. Feasts do not replace Sundays, solemnities, Ash Wednesday, or any day within the Triduum or Octave of Easter.

A **memorial** can be either optional or obligatory. For Morning and Evening Prayer, an obligatory memorial begins with the current weekday for the psalms and canticle unless there are psalms or antiphons included in the Proper of Saints. For the remainder of these hours, refer to the Proper of Saints and/or Commons. For some saints, there might only be a proper concluding prayer.

Optional memorials are celebrations of

saints, but it's up to you whether to observe that celebration or stick with the current weekday in the current season of Ordinary Time or Advent. They are celebrated in the same way as obligatory memorials. (During Lent, optional memorials can be observed as commemorations; this means you only use the prayer from the Proper of Saints. Everything else is taken from the current weekday of Lent.)

In a breviary or liturgical calendar printed in the United States, obligatory memorials are designated "memorial" and optional memorials have no designation.

10
Group Prayer

The Liturgy of the Hours wasn't originally meant to be prayed by individuals on their own; it was designed to be prayed in common. Praying the Hours aloud with a community, spouse, or friend is very different from praying silently on your own. It also comes with its own set of challenges that you don't experience with solo prayer.

As you pray the psalms in the Liturgy of the Hours, you'll notice that they're broken up into stanzas, called *strophes*. When praying in common, alternate these strophes: If only two people are praying, take turns reading them; if more than two are praying, divide the room into two groups that will take turns reading in unison.

Before you begin praying, establish how the following roles will be filled:

- The *leader* or *presider* begins the opening verse ("God, come to my assistance"), reads the prayer at the end of each psalm (if those optional prayers are being used), leads the intercessions (more on that below), begins the Lord's Prayer, and reads the closing prayer.
- The *antiphonarian* reads the antiphons before and after each psalm or canticle and begins the first line of the first verse of each psalm or canticle; one group joins in on the second line, and the second group takes its turn at the beginning of the next strophe. The groups alternate reciting strophes until the end of the psalm or canticle.
- The *reader* reads the reading

> and begins the responsory (the full community responds in unison).

The group will also need to decide how the intercessions will be handled. They are written in two-part format, but the Church leaves it up to individual communities to decide whether the presider will read each intention in full with the congregation using a stock response, or stop at the break so that the congregation responds with the second part of the intention.

The biggest challenge when praying in community is the need for consistency. When different members of the praying community use different formats or sources for the prayers, it can get very confusing. Someone praying from *Shorter Christian Prayer* will find it difficult to pray with someone else who is using a four-volume breviary, in many cases. And those who use apps or periodicals to pray may find that the format they're using doesn't match the format of the printed breviary. It's best, in a group setting, to find a common format everyone can use, regardless of the one he or she usually uses in personal prayer.

11
Quick-Start Guide

1. **Start small.** The easiest of the Hours to learn is Night Prayer. It's unique among the Hours because it only has one week's rotation of prayers. All you need to know to pray Night Prayer is what day it is. Night Prayer is a beautiful way to end the day — and if you would like to pray the Liturgy of the Hours as a family, Night Prayer is an excellent place to begin.
2. **Start on Saturday evening.** The new week begins with Evening Prayer I for Sunday. You'll find that as you begin Week I with

Evening Prayer I (on Saturday evening) there are directions in red ink to help guide you through the ritual.

3. **Set up the ribbons first.** Have you ever arrived early enough at church to see the priest or deacon finding the correct pages in the lectionary and sacramentary, and marking them with ribbons? Get yourself set up before you begin praying the Liturgy of the Hours each day, in just the same way. This isn't an issue on a regular Wednesday in Ordinary Time, but when you're in a special season (Advent, Lent, or Easter) or observing a saint's feast day, there will be multiple pages to mark. When I finish praying one Hour, I like to get my ribbons and other page markers in their plac-

es for the next one. This way, when that time rolls around, I can simply open the book and begin to pray. Try this — you'll thank yourself in the morning.

4. **Keep an eye on the calendar.** Check the liturgical calendar at the beginning of the week and note what's coming up. Solemnities begin with Evening Prayer I on the day before, just as Sundays do, so it helps to plan ahead.
5. **Know where to find the canticle.** Morning and Evening Prayer both include Gospel canticles. Your breviary may have included cards with those canticles printed on them, but you can also find them at the beginning of the section of the breviary called the Ordinary, which contains all the basic prayers and procedures.

6. **Say the black, do the red.** The red type indicates what part of the Hour you are on: psalm, canticle, reading, responsory, Gospel canticle, intercessions, or prayer. You don't read the words in red; they are simply there to guide you. Also, the italicized sentence beneath the title and description of each psalm or canticle is there for private meditation and is not spoken aloud.
7. **Skip the psalm-prayer.** This is the prayer at the end of each psalm in Morning and Evening Prayer. These prayers are actually optional, and are not included in editions of the breviary outside the United States.

12
SOS!

Where do I put all these ribbons?

The ribbons are bookmarks, but it's up to you how you use them. Even though I taught my husband how to pray Liturgy of the Hours, he has worked out a different system for ribbon use than I have. And that's fine — the ribbons are tools for you to use in the way that works best for you. Personally, I keep one ribbon in the current spot in the Proper of Seasons, one in the four-week Psalter, one in the current day of the week for Night Prayer, one in the Proper of Saints, and the last one in the Common of Saints.

I've run out of ribbons before I've run out of prayers!

That's what holy cards are for. I always keep a few holy cards in the back of my breviary and deploy them when the ribbons aren't enough. I also use a holy card to mark the page for the Invitatory psalm, and another as a placeholder for Sunday, Morning Prayer, Week I, because the psalms and canticles for that day are also used for for every solemnity and feast.

Glory — or Glory *Be*?

This brief prayer of praise to the Trinity is known as the *doxology.* It concludes every psalm and canticle — unless you are directed otherwise — and is included in the introduction to most Hours and in part in the responsory. But in the current translation of the Liturgy of the Hours, the doxology uses slightly different wording from the Glory Be you likely use in praying the Rosary:

Glory to the Father and to the Son
and to the Holy Spirit.
— As it was in the beginning, is
now and will be forever. Amen.

Sit, stand, or kneel?

Prayer posture is important: We can see that during Mass, we stand and kneel at certain times to show our reverence for the Gospel and for the holy Eucharist on the altar. In much the same way, when groups pray Liturgy of the Hours, it's customary to stand during the Gospel canticle. The rest of the time, sitting is an appropriate posture.

Which prayers should I use to celebrate the Blessed Virgin Mary?

The Common of the Blessed Virgin Mary is used on any feast of the Blessed Mother. Some feasts have more proper content than others; for example, the prayers on the solemnity of the Assumption of the Blessed Virgin Mary are not exactly the same as the prayers on the optional memorial of

Our Lady of Fatima. There is much more proper content for the Assumption. But on both of these feasts, and all other feasts of the Blessed Virgin Mary, you will include some elements from this section in your prayer.

The memorial of the Blessed Virgin Mary on Saturday offers an antiphon for the Invitatory and various alternatives for the readings, responsory, antiphon for the Gospel canticle, intercessions, and prayer to be used during Morning Prayer. As this is only prayed on Saturdays, which is the day traditionally dedicated to the Blessed Mother, no Evening Prayer content is needed; Saturday evenings are always Evening Prayer I for Sunday. This Saturday celebration is an optional memorial that can be chosen during Ordinary Time, both at daily Mass for Saturday and in the Liturgy of the Hours. If another feast is not already celebrated on that date, the first Saturday of the month would be a particularly appropriate time to pray this optional memorial.

I pray the Liturgy of the Hours alone. Do I need to pray out loud?

The Liturgy of the Hours, which originated as a form of common prayer, was intended to be prayed out loud. If you are praying alone, you do not need to pray aloud. But you always have that option, should you wish to do so. Praying aloud can help you slow down if you find that you're zipping through the psalms and not paying attention.

I forgot to pray Morning Prayer, and now it's 2:00 p.m.! What do I do?

Only priests and deacons are required to pray the Liturgy of the Hours. If you're a priest or deacon, you'll need to pray Morning Prayer at 2:00 p.m. if you didn't do so earlier. Otherwise, be gentle with yourself. Pray Midafternoon Prayer right now, or make a firm resolution to pick up again at Evening Prayer.

I just realized I prayed the wrong prayers for this Hour!

This happens. Maybe you left your ribbon in the wrong place. Maybe you woke up convinced it was Thursday but it was really Wednesday. Maybe you forgot it was a feast day. Maybe you grabbed the wrong card for the Gospel canticle. Maybe you got all the way to the Gospel canticle before realizing you were praying Evening Prayer at 6:00 a.m. (Yes, I have done all of these.)

If you're partway through an Hour and you figure out that you're in the wrong spot, pause and find the right one, and continue from where you are. Don't backtrack to the beginning. If you've finished the Hour and then realized you should have done something different, you don't need to re-pray the correct Hour.

Consider it a learning experience. And try setting up your ribbons the night before. That way, when you begin to pray in the morning, everything is ready for you. After you finish Morning Prayer, set up your ribbons for Evening Prayer, and so on.

Each Hour contains at least one hymn. Do I need to sing them?

The Hymn is actually part of the prayer for each Hour, so it shouldn't be skipped. However, you don't necessarily have to sing it. You can chant the lyrics, if you prefer, or simply recite them. Another option is listening to a recording of the hymn.

The psalms are so militaristic. I don't like thinking about God that way.

There are many references to military glory in the psalms. That's to be expected, when you consider that David was a soldier and then a king, the military leader of his nation — as well as the composer of many of the psalms. We write from what we know, and King David was no different. In some of the psalms he petitions God to defend him from enemies, which are portrayed in military terms; today, we'd probably describe our enemies in different ways, but we have no less need of God's protecting hand. The psalms don't glorify war or the loss of life that comes along with war — they glorify God as protector, defender, and deliverer, and as the only bringer of true peace.

It's so repetitive!

Think of the Liturgy of the Hours as "familiar" rather than "repetitive." You will find, as you build the habit of praying the Liturgy of the Hours, that every four weeks — and sometimes more frequently than that — you'll encounter the same psalms or readings. The Gospel canticles are the same every day. But repetition doesn't have to be a problem. The psalms and prayers and readings included in the Liturgy of the Hours were carefully curated to lead the faithful to God.

Praying the same psalms and canticles again and again will help you learn them by heart — a term I prefer to the word *memorize* because you're praying, not cramming for a final exam. As you pray a prayer or psalm again and again, you'll gradually need to look at the page less and less, as the words simply begin to flow.

Repetition can also be very comforting. Think about a little child who wants to hear the same bedtime story every night — sometimes several times a night. That story has become part of her routine, and hearing it daily is comforting to her. You, too, will begin to find comfort in the ever more familiar words of psalms and readings that you use to offer praise, glory, thanksgiving, and petition to God. And you'll begin to find favorite elements that seem to come up right when you need them. For me, one of those occurs in Morning Prayer on Tuesdays of Weeks I and III: "My God stands by me, all my trust is in him." Coming upon those words from Scripture that you find most comforting is truly a gift, one that you can unwrap multiple times a day when you pray the Liturgy of the Hours.

13
You Can Do It!

The Liturgy of the Hours is a beautiful way to pray with the universal Church — whether you pray in a group or alone. While it can be daunting at first, you learn as you go along, and you'll find spiritual nourishment in the prayers, psalms, and other Scripture passages. And you'll be following the examples of centuries of saints as you pray in union with the saints-to-be of today's Church.

As you begin to pray the Liturgy of the Hours, resolve to be patient with yourself as you learn. The rewards of this type of prayer are great, and you won't have to wait until heaven to begin to reap them.

About the Author

Barb Szyszkiewicz is a wife, mother of three young adults, a music minister at her parish, and a Secular Franciscan. She is editor at CatholicMom.com and blogs at FranciscanMom.com. Barb enjoys writing, cooking, and reading, and is the author of *The Handy Little Guide to Prayer.*

You might also like:

The Handy Little Guide to Spiritual Communion

By Michael R. Heinlein

There is a lot of information online about the practice of spiritual communion, not all of which you might find helpful. So you might be wondering: Is spiritual communion just something between me and Jesus? Is spiritual communion of no value if I can't receive the Eucharist? Is spiritual communion "just" a private prayer or devotion? (It's none of those things.)

Sometimes we may be unable to attend Mass or receive the Eucharist. That's why it's important for Catholics to understand and practice spiritual communion. Gain clarity, comfort, and encouragement in this brief booklet.